To: Chr
Enjoy
all your endeavors
your friend,
Michael Mavias

CREATING VALUE

By Creating Continually Improving Cash Value

MICHAEL G. MAVIAS

PublishAmerica
Baltimore

First printing

ISBN: 1-4137-9113-1
PUBLISHED BY PUBLISHAMERICA, LLLP
www.publishamerica.com
Baltimore

Printed in the United States of America

Dedicated to my wife, Mary Mavias, who has supported me for forty-two years, and who encouraged me to write this book.

TABLE OF CONTENTS

PREFACE

Over the years many books and articles have been written about specific segments of the business that companies and organizations need to improve on to create value, such as customer service, strategy, proper involvement of people in the company, new product or service introduction, re-engineering of existing products or services, developing a lean enterprise, cycle time reduction, quality improvement, creating value for your customer, supplier, employee and investor, safety programs, ethical behavior, profitable growth, operational efficiency, asset utilization and continuous improvement as a way of life, to name a few.

I decided, after much thought about many of the aforementioned topics, that a book evaluating the processes and systems which create cash value in any company or organization would be extremely useful to anyone attempting to provide a product or service to their customers. At times, in a corporate or private environment, employees and executives alike sometimes forget that they are only in business to create value and positive cash flow for the organization's owners. These are two absolutes, whether you are a privately held or a public company, a manufacturer of goods, a deliverer of services, a for profit company with stockholders or a non-profit company with clients. Value growth and cash flow are the life-blood of any organization. This book was written with the goal in mind of creating positive cash flow and adding value to any organization. It basically revolves around the theme of creating value for your customer, supplier, employee and investor in order to be successful. To do so, you must have a sound business strategy and business plan, understood by all employees and formed within your business environment. The business strategy must be attainable within the realm of the organization's existence and be demanding enough to maintain profitable growth, operational efficiencies and asset utilization in order to create positive cash flow value and economic profit. To maintain success, no level of success is ever completely satisfactory. If you plan on creating value added and continually improving cash flow, continuously improving in all areas of your business is an absolute.

Where to start? Try looking at your major costs and see where total labor costs are positioned on your financial reports. Companies need to recognize that their people are the foundation of everything they do. People truly are any organization's #1 asset and, in many cases, the number one cost, and should be treated as such. Many companies honor the #1 philosophy until any one of a hundred expedient solutions occurs. They do not walk the talk. In my opinion, unless your people strategy is the foundation of everything that you do, you can not be successful in value creation. I have dedicated a portion of the book to creative people strategies and various organizations' attempts at strategic and operational planning.

In conclusion, I feel that this book can be used as an excellent reference manual for you on how to create and perpetuate positive cash flow value for your company or organization.

INTRODUCTION

Creating Continually Improving Cash Value

The ultimate goal of most companies is to be world class competitive. But what is the world in which they compete and with whom are they competing? What are their markets, products, plans, capabilities, desires, strengths, and weaknesses? What is success? We will look at many aspects of the issues facing large and small employers in an environment which, at best, is a mix of known unknowns. As I discuss many of the issues I have experienced, I will do so from a reality base; theory is best left in our colleges, universities and consulting firms. I will try to discuss the realities of what it means for an organization to be the best in the world in which they are competing. In order to try to accomplish this, I hope to describe, in specific terms, how organizations can provide a vehicle for the creation and maintenance of a balanced value for their customers, suppliers, employees and investors. Any organization's ultimate goal should be to ensure that customers, suppliers, employees and investors are all successful. Most companies agree that people are their #1 asset, but their actions do not support this theory. I shall show you how to utilize your people to ensure that you are creating maximum cash value.

In order to accomplish this you must plan to continuously improve on profitable growth, operational efficiency and asset utilization. In world class companies continuous improvement is a way of life. Companies that target improved market share that is not profitable will not be successful. That is purely growth for growth's sake. Also, costs must continually be managed at all levels of the operation, and assets must be fully utilized in order to be successful.

The ultimate goal should be continuous improvement and predictability in your forecasts and actual cash flows and positive economic profits. The way to accomplish this is to totally understand your business environment, have a vision and strategy that is understood and embraced by all, have a world class plan to accomplish your goals and to ensure that you are creating continually improving cash value for your customers, suppliers, employees and investors.

CHAPTER I

Understand Your Business Environment

Markets—world class companies have a clear understanding of what business they are in and understand the markets for their products/ services. They focus on what they do best in order to continually create and increase value. Since they must do business in an environment that is extremely complex and volatile, they must operate with the flexibility to adapt quickly to changes. As "all politics are local politics" may reflect on our political system, so does the concept of "all business is local business" reflect on all business environments. We must understand the environment we operate within, have strategies for coping with it, and have the resolve to act, if we are going to have a world class organization, regardless of the world in which we operate. An illustration of this concept is a company in Tiffin,

Ohio—National Machinery [i]. National Machinery is the world leader in the design, development, and manufacture of cold, warm, and hot forming machines that produce metal parts from coiled wire, bars, slugs, or preforms. Through their continuing research and development, advanced manufacturing capability and worldwide network of sales and service locations, National Machinery has firmly established its position as the "World Standard for Excellence" in cold forming machinery technology. Their stated objective is "the satisfaction of customers' needs with high-quality products, technology, and services while achieving above-average profitability and maintaining a rewarding environment for employees. Products, technology, and services must surpass competition in meeting worldwide customer needs. We are judged by the performance of our products. Profits are the measure of how efficiently we provide our customers the best products. Profits provide a fair return to our owners and are required to survive and grow. People are the source of our strength. Knowledge, involvement and teamwork are essential to our success."

Create Value for External/Internal Customers

World class organizations have a clear understanding of who their customers are. This includes External and

Internal customers, since everyone in a company is both a customer and a supplier. They also determine what a customer really wants and develop and execute a plan for the organization to totally support customer requirements in order to ensure full customer satisfaction. Also, they develop and continually improve reliable processes focused on value added, waste elimination and simplification and improved quality in order to keep focused on their customers. Quality in a product or service is not what the supplier puts in; it is what the customer gets out of it and is willing to pay for. Customers pay only for what is of use to them and gives them value. World class companies are partners with their customers. They communicate with, listen to and involve them in the design/redesign of products/services that create value for them. An example of this is when Boeing[ii] decided to build the 777. Customers were brought in and asked what type of aircraft would be suitable for their future needs. After much discussion and redesign, the 777 was born, and it has been a highly successful aircraft. This approach works in all sectors of the economy, whether it is manufacturing or service. Why provide a product or service that your customers do not want? Remember, you need to create value for your customers in order for you to be successful.

Another example of creating value for your customers is the Paris Coffee Shop in Fort Worth, Texas, which has been in existence for 77 years and is owned and operated by Mike Smith.

Customers come from all over the state of Texas and the United States to enjoy his Texas hospitality and home-cooked breakfasts and lunches. Mike says his success comes from being able to change with the times. The trend to healthier eating influenced a light menu, which has been a big success. Mike enjoys talking with customers about eating healthier. "Many of our customers are taking up eating lighter so they can enjoy a piece of pie without feeling so guilty." The homemade pies and heat-sealed right-out-of-the oven-flavored cookies, in addition to Mike's high quality menu offerings and outstanding customer service, entice repeat customers. Jane and Michael Stern, editors of the "Taste of America: Road Food and Good Food" column in the *St. Louis Post,* visited several years ago and wrote the sentiments of many who eat here regularly. "Eating the pie at Paris Coffee Shop is one of America's distinctive culinary experiences. Pie and coffee in a home-cooking café, after all, is as American as well, apple pie."

"We have the broadest range of clientele you'll find anywhere, from families to construction crews to bankers, actors and sports figures", Smith said.

Whether you are manufacturing a product or providing a service, you must always create value for your customers in order to be successful. This is the formula for success, whether it be manufacturing airplanes or running a coffee shop.

This approach also works on internal customers. You should continually encourage coordinated and cooperative cross-functional operations. If you are providing a product/service to someone else in the organization you should ensure that you are giving them a product/service with zero defects and providing them with on-time delivery so they can be successful. This team approach will lead to the creation of value for all. An illustration of this may best be found from one of the world's leading manufacturers of automobiles, BMW[iii]. The recent change over from the Z-3 to the Z-4, in BMW's Spartanburg, South Carolina plant found over 70% of the process improvements coming from the operating employees, and from BMW people comes truly an excellent summary "from great minds come great products."

Another example of understanding your customers' needs is a finance organization that should provide all pertinent financial data on time, with no defects, to all their internal and external customers. Also, they should only provide financial data that their internal and external customers deem valuable and necessary, not what the finance organization feels their customers should receive. Internal customers should be surveyed to determine what data they feel creates value for them.

You should continually strive to deliver products/ services when your customers require them and ensure they are technically excellent and have zero defects. The goal should be that the product/service will outlast the warranty period.

The post-sale service cycle which provides service to the customer is as important as the product itself and must be treated as such. An example of this is how top notch automobile dealers handle their customers. After the sale of the automobile is completed they ensure that the customers receive first class service on any warranty claims on their automobiles. In addition, they provide total service capability for their customers' maintenance needs, such as oil changes, brakes, tires, etc., so that customers do not have to go elsewhere for any of their automotive needs. By providing total service for all their customer needs, the dealer is increasing their cash value and also providing value to the customer. This also will increase the possibility of the customer being a repeat customer when they are in the market for a new or used vehicle, since they are being provided the product that they want, which is of superior quality at a competitive price, and are being provided world class service for their vehicle as long as they own the vehicle.

In addition, world class companies develop metrics and other means to truly measure customer satisfaction. One way of accomplishing this is to set up creating value measurements for your customers, to measure: 1. On-time delivery performance 2. Defects-quality performance 3. Cycle time improvement and 4. A customer survey to measure how the customer rates your performance against their requirements.

In order to become and remain a world class company you must continually evaluate your competition and take advantage of all opportunities. By providing value and satisfying your customers you will stay ahead of your competitors.

If you are continually improving your cash value you should be able to provide extremely competitive pricing for your products/services, which means that you will experience profitable growth and improving cash flows.

CHAPTER II

Translating Your Strategy into Action

Strategic planning is an ongoing process and carries an intense customer focus. The strategic plan drives decisions and actions. Employees at all levels should be able to articulate and embrace the company's vision and strategic direction. The company must have an obsession with excellence; there is dissatisfaction with the status quo. Executives should provide the leadership necessary for change. They must articulate the motivations for positive change and other core values, and communicate them widely throughout the organization by actions as well as by words. Employees are truly recognized as the company's #1 asset.

There is an explicit written business strategy that includes a vision and articulates the commitment to excellence and the overriding importance of customer satisfaction.

The company continuously measures its products, services and practices against the toughest competitors, within and outside of the industry, and recognizes the principle of sustainable competitive advantage. This information is used to identify "best practices" and establish performance benchmarks.

A business planning process is used to develop and communicate annual financial plans that incorporate input from all operating segments of the company.

Develop a vision—Where are we going?

Back in the 1960s, President John F. Kennedy had a vision that was communicated to all Americans. It was that we were going to land a man on the moon by the end of the decade. A vision must be clear and communicated and understood by all if you are going to be successful. In this case, we did land an American on the moon by the end of the decade.

At a shipbuilders' conference in Seattle, Washington, a vision for one of the shipbuilders was to be the best shipyard in the world and to become the shipyard of choice for commercial and Navy customers.

An organization within a company can also have a vision, which would support the company vision. For example, the vision for a finance organization could be that they become a finance organization with the best services, value and people.

The end result of any business vision should be to provide increasing economic returns to your employees and shareholders, by continually improving your cash flow value.

Develop a strategy—How do we get there?

To attain the vision, you must develop a solid business and product/service strategy, and if you are a manufacturing company, a production strategy, and utilize *Creating Value* techniques to translate the vision and strategy into a set of objectives and measures. The strategy should render choices about what not to do as well as choices about what needs to be accomplished if you are to be successful. Deciding which target group of customers, products and services should be provided and needs the company should serve is fundamental to developing a sound strategy. You must decide what you are going to be when you grow up and what your market niche is; you cannot be everything to everybody and must decide which customers not to serve and which products or services not to offer. One of the most important functions of an explicit, communicated strategy is to guide employees in making good business choices that when handled properly will create value.

In the case of John F. Kennedy, the United States would develop and manufacture a world class spacecraft capable of landing a man on the moon by the end of the decade.

To be the best shipyard in the world, this shipyard would set the standard for on-time delivery, product quality and cost.

To become the best finance organization, customer-valued information and financial data would be provided with highly skilled and motivated people.

To become the best you must use lean techniques (which I will describe more under strategic objectives) to create value and translate them into your business environment and develop a comprehensive business and financial plan that will lead to profitable growth. This will be accomplished as you set the standard for on-time delivery, product/service quality, and low inventory and continue to have successes through aggressive, continuous process improvements which lead to the elimination of waste, with significant reductions in product/process costs, which will maximize operational efficiencies. This, coupled with improved asset utilization, will generate a positive cash flow and improved shareholder value and economic profit.

Develop strategic objectives— What do we need to do well?

Utilize value stream mapping to map out the current processes as to how the employees are actually performing their jobs. This is not flow chart mapping of how you think the operation is run. Then, map out new processes, eliminating all non-value-added activities that do not pertain to the business, product/service, production and people strategy. Your objectives should pertain to improving speed, flexibility and quality by eliminating waste items which are non-value-added activities. Examples of some of these would be:

The waste of complexity – Find simple solutions in place of complex ones. Complex solutions produce more waste and are harder for people to manage.

The waste of labor – Eliminate all unnecessary movements and steps of people.

The waste of overproduction – Produce only the exact amount of goods or services the customer wants when the customer wants them. Eliminate any production beyond customer demand.

The waste of space – Conserve space in the plant or office layout by improving arrangement of machines, people, workstations, storage, work in process and raw material and finished goods inventory.

The waste of energy – Operate equipment and use person-power only for productive purposes. Avoid false scale efficiencies, excess power utilization and unproductive operations.

The waste of defects – Set a goal of no rework ever (no mistakes, recycles, rework and defects).

The waste of materials – Convert all raw into products. Avoid scrap, trim, excess, or bad raw material.

The waste of idle materials – Make sure nothing sits so there is a steady flow to the customer. Any idle excess or obsolete inventory represents waste (raw material, work in process, information, finished goods).

The waste of time – Eliminate delays, long set-ups and unplanned downtime of machines, processes or people. Set up a preventative maintenance program to eliminate the unplanned downtime.

The waste of transportation – Eliminate the movement of materials or information that does not add value to the product or service.

Lean Enterprise

Your objectives should tie in to the aggressive implementation of tools and techniques which will permit you to incorporate lean production, repair and service as you eliminate waste. Lean production is a manufacturing system based on the Toyota production model, where closely coupled manufacturing systems characterized by very low inventory and first-time quality remove much of the non-value-added work and reduce costs. The term 'lean' was coined by investigators from MIT in a book entitled *The Machine that Changed the World* [Womack et al., 1990] in which they assert that a lean production system involves one-half the human effort in the factory, one-half the manufacturing space, one-half the investment tools, one-half the engineering hours and one-half the time to develop new products.

Lean practices involve elimination of waste on the shop floor, in the office, in supplier management, in inventory management, in design and development of products/services, in all your human resource people activities and so forth. Eliminating excess and obsolete inventory, for example, drives closer linkages between assemblers and suppliers, reshapes the factory floor and forces greater attention to first-time quality. Attention to zero-defect quality, cycle time reduction and product/service flow drives costs down throughout the production/service process, from the design phase through final delivery to the customer, creating value for the customers, people, suppliers and investors. Tailored tools and techniques facilitate the systematic and continued search for non-value-added activities and sources of waste.

Transforming a manufacturing/service operation to a lean environment constitutes a re-engineering of the entire process as a closely interconnected system from which buffers are removed. The synergies from applying lean to different areas of the process are so significant that while isolated implementation efforts can result in impressive gains, these represent a small fraction of what full-scale implementation would offer. Consequently, the associated organizational and coordination requirements make implementing lean a difficult and complex endeavor, but one that is worthwhile if you are truly dedicated to creating increasing value for your business. A lean strategy should be designed to increase velocity in order to improve flexibility in responding to customers required delivery dates, eliminate waste and minimize or eliminate process variation in order to do things right the first time.

One way to accomplish the elimination of process variation is to combine a Six Sigma quality program with Lean Initiatives. Leading the Six Sigma program are "black belts" who have had intensive training in statistical methods and team leadership. Utilizing Six Sigma techniques, they can assist in generating the data needed to justify major changes, including equipment upgrades, where needed. Six Sigma tools, such as cause and effect analysis, often play a key role in getting the kinks out of a lean system by pinpointing the causes of process variation.

A central thrust in becoming lean in a manufacturing environment is the development of lean production cells in order to improve on-time delivery and quality performance. The conversion to lean cells requires development of a co-located multi-skilled workforce—hourly and exempt. These employees function as a team and are trained to handle many jobs, as required. This results in improved employee productivity, which creates value and helps secure their jobs in the future.

In order for employees to be productive, the facility must be re-engineered to incorporate a lean process flow. Work stations, work instructions and tools must be standardized and organized for maximum efficiency of use. Employees should utilize ergonomic chairs and workstations to reduce or eliminate work-related injuries. An overhead power grid should be installed to improve flexibility when a cell is re-organized. Tests should be incorporated into the process and test equipment should be part of the cell. Receiving and inspection should be eliminated and with the help of the Six Sigma program and the "black belts," employees will be responsible for first pass quality and zero defects at the source. The processes should be improved to the point of making it impossible to do it wrong the first time.

In order to ensure that material required is available, point of use storage bins (child bins) should be co-located in the cell and replenished with a kanban pull system. When inventory of a part is depleted, demand is transferred to a main storage bin (mother bin), where the stock is replenished. This then creates demand for a re-order of parts, as required.

For pull production (A) item parts, the supplier manufactures to a stable agreed to forecast and keeps consigned inventory in the plant to replenish the mother bins.

For auto-replenishment (B) items, the supplier holds

90 days of bonded inventory based on a long-range forecast which is sent monthly to the supplier and is authorized by a blanket purchase order with "as required" schedules. Deliveries are based on shop consumption.

For on-site stores (C) items, which are high-part count or high-maintenance commodities, the supplier maintains a bonded inventory and delivers the material "as required."

By working with suppliers as partners, parts availability and quality will be improved and inventory will be reduced as you will not be required to carry as much inventory, since your suppliers will not charge you for inventory that they are keeping in their stock room in your facility until you require it.

In a lean environment, the product line is fully integrated, with minimal handoffs, pre-positioned material and utilizes a multi-skilled workforce.

Set up creating value measures

How do we measure how well we are doing? Set up business unit and company creating value measures for customers (external and internal), suppliers, people and investors. Each support group should also have their own creating value measures and behave like service companies. They should have objectives, strategies and a linkage scorecard that ties in and helps them focus on better service to the business units. All business and support group creating value measures should tell the story of the company strategy and should be part of a chain of cause and effect linkages that roll up to the overall company strategic objectives. Also, every measure should ultimately tie in to financial results and the creation of continually improving cash value. A balance should exist between outcome measures and performance drivers which will redefine a process to eliminate non-value-added activities or change behavior.

Customer Measures (external and internal)—Measure:

1. On-time delivery performance based on the date the customer requires the delivery. Some customers may also require a certain time of the day for delivery to the receiving dock.

2. Defects-quality performance based on zero defects.

3. Cycle time improvement based on when you receive the order for the product/service to when you deliver it to the customer.

4. A customer survey to measure how the customer rates your performance against their requirements. External and internal customers should be measured separately.

Supplier Measures—Measure:

1. On-time delivery performance to you based on your requirements of when you require the delivery.

2. Defects-quality performance. All products/services delivered to you should have zero defects and require no inspection on your part.

3. Cost performance—All products/services contracted for delivery to you should be extremely competitively priced.

4. Customer Satisfaction—Your suppliers should be given feedback on your satisfaction with their products/services and scored accordingly.

Employee Measures—Measure:

1. Performance management—All employees should have a signed off performance management/individual development improvement plan.

2. Recognition—Recognize/reward people for attainment of initiatives.

3. Attrition—Measure unwanted attrition.

4. Employee survey—Conduct once a year. Measure employee satisfaction.

Financial/Investor Measures – Measure:

1. Scrap/rework/warranty costs to determine if your first pass/zero defect quality program is working.

2. Productivity improvement—Measure the impact of producing and delivering increased products/services with the same or less people.

3. Measure your inventory accuracy by utilizing cycle counts. Your physical inventory and stock status counts should match, if accurate, and your costing valuation of the inventory should match what your books show as your inventory amount. Measure inventory turns. This is yearly cost of sales/average inventory. Measure excess/ obsolete inventory based on past, present and forecasted demand. You should only keep inventory that will be used in a pre-determined time period such as two prior years' usage and three forecasted years.

4. Measure the forecast accuracy of your formal planning and scheduling system in order to continuously improve the process. This process is used for forecasting all anticipated demands with sufficient detail and an adequate planning horizon to support business planning,

sales and operations planning, and master production scheduling.

5. Measure the accuracy of your bills of material and routing or operation sheets if you are manufacturing a product. Part numbers, descriptions and quantities must be accurate on the bills of material and represent the parts required to manufacture the product. Labor run and set-up standards, quantities and operations must be accurate on the routing or operation sheets.

6. Measure return on sales = Net earnings after tax/by net sales.

7. Measure return on net assets employed (RONA) = Operating earnings/average net assets.

8. Measure asset turns = Yearly cost of goods sold/Average net assets.

9. Measure cash flow = Net earnings +/- change in net assets: When forecasting future cash flows, calculate the net present value of cash adjusted for inflation. This is known as discounted cash flow.

10. Measure free cash flow = Net earnings +/- non cash adj. (I.E. depreciation expense) adjusted for inflation = Cash earnings +/- change in working capital.

11. Measure economic profit = After tax earnings less an estimated capital charge of 5-15% of your average net assets depending on the current cost of capital.

12. Measure shareholder value = Shares of stock outstanding x stock market price.

13. Measure earnings per share = (Net earnings after tax divided by number of shares outstanding).

Set up targets—What level of performance is required in order to be successful?

Set strategic and tactical stretch targets for the level of performance required to be successful for profitable growth and predictable and improved cash flow. Communicate these performance targets to all employees and ensure by-in. Listen to suggestions from your people for improvements to objectives, measures and the stretch targets. Empower them to incorporate changes, where applicable. These profitable growth, operational efficiency, asset utilization and cash flow targets can form the basis for a supplemental reward (bonus) system that would tie rewards/recognition to the attainment of stretch targets that lead to improved cash flow and shareholder value.

Some examples of stretch targets are as follows:

1. Customer/supplier delivery performance—Delivery performance should be 95-100% of the customer-required date.

2. Customer/supplier quality performance—Quality performance should be 98-100% with the standard target being zero defects on products or services delivered to the customer or by the supplier.

3. Scrap, rework and recycles as a percent of sales should be less than 2%, with 0% being the ultimate stretch target.

4. Cycle time improvement—Set targets that will cause the organization to stretch each year as you continually eliminate waste and reduce your flow times with the ultimate goal being the elimination of all non-value-added activities.

5. Productivity targets should be set for continuous improvement each year with the stretch target of 100% productivity being the goal.

6. Formal planning and scheduling system accuracy should be in the 95-100% range.

7. Inventory accuracy—at least 95% of all item inventory records should match the physical counts, within the counting tolerance.

8. Inventory turns—Set stretch targets each year to continually improve your turns and cash flow.

9. Bill of material and routing structure and accuracy should be in the 95-100 % range.

10. Return on sales, return on net assets employed and current and future cash flow should be targeted as continually improving, with predictability and forecast accuracy also being a goal.

11. Economic profit should be targeted as always remaining positive and improving. This will occur as long as you continually have a positive return on sales and are maximizing the utilization of your net assets.

Develop people strategy initiatives—How do we support achieving our targets?

World class organizations value and develop a committed, competent and empowered workforce. Trust, teamwork, mutual respect, open communications and a high degree of job security are hallmarks of the employee/company relationship. Employees are very pleased with the company and proud to be a part of it. Everything accomplished in an organization is a result of actions by those people. World class organizations develop a partnership with their employees, properly train and motivate them, develop two-way communication with them, empower them and reward and recognize them so they will engage in continuous productive improvement activities which will provide a competitive advantage. Technology, product, capital assets and facilities are useless without people. People are critical to attaining and sustaining world class levels of performance and are a source of competitive advantage, since the success of the organization is linked to the well-being of its people. The more competent, committed and flexible the members of the organization, the more flexible and competent is the company. In world class organizations, the only fear employees should face is the fear that outside competition may service their customers better.

Management at world class organizations realize that people play a crucial role in the ultimate success of the company and have a commitment to treating people with dignity, trust, openness, honesty and respect, communicating to them with their actions that they are the organizations' #1 asset, and providing constructive feedback as a highly valued and demonstrated organizational trait. Teams are used to multiply the strength of the organization and are used as the primary means to address specific objectives, organize the work, and develop initiatives that will be required to support achieving the targets that have been established, as opposed to individual employees working at independent work stations handling this assignment. People are empowered to take direct action, make decisions, and initiate changes by developing initiatives that will permit the organization to achieve agreed to targets and to support the strategic objectives which will create positive cash flow value.

Performance management

Performance management is used as a tool with each employee to indicate the contribution the employee must make in order for the organization to be successful in attaining the vision, strategy and strategic objectives that have been agreed to by all the employees. When the objectives, measures, targets and initiatives have been successfully attained, reward and recognize the teams and individuals that completed the initiatives that tie in to the company vision, strategy and objectives. Also, the targets for current and projected earnings, positive cash flow and economic profit must be met in order to pay out any supplemental bonus arrangements based on a large scale gain sharing program incentive award system, if one is available.

As part of performance management, each employee should be required to have an individual development and improvement plan which will contribute to them continuing to be the #1 asset of the company. An active education and training process for all employees should be in place focused on business and customer issues and improvements. Its objectives include continuous improvement, enhancing the empowered worker, flexibility, employment stability and meeting future needs.

Set up people creating value measures and targets

100% of employees must have a performance management and individual development and improvement plan that details the commitment the employee is making to continually improve and to attainment of various initiatives that are an integral part of the company vision, strategy and objectives. These must be reviewed with each employee at least twice a year. There should be two way written and verbal communication at this meeting with the manager and employee each expressing their thoughts on how well the employee is performing to the plan.

Reward/recognize achievements towards completion of initiatives that support achieving agreed to targets. A simple form of recognition could be "Thank you for a job well done."

Measure attrition—A goal could be that unwanted attrition should not exceed 10%.

Set up communication meetings with employees.

Performance management—Review twice a year.

Staff meetings—Conduct monthly.

All employee meetings—Conduct monthly. Review business plan results at this meeting, recognize team and individual contributions for completion of initiatives, communicate any major changes to the business plan and permit time for employees to ask questions or discuss issues that concern them.

Distribute and review business plan results monthly.

Employee survey—Conduct once a year. Establish focus groups to work on specific tasks identified for improvement from the company survey. Review results with employees quarterly in the all employee meeting.

In summary, your people strategy is the most important part of your plan. If you state that people are your #1 asset and don't walk the talk you will not have a world class company. People are the foundation of any business and should always be treated as your #1 asset. You must totally communicate with, engage in a partnership complete with mutual respect, honesty and trust, provide empowerment opportunities, and reward and recognize people for completion of initiatives that tie-in to the company vision, strategies and objectives if you are to be successful in continuing to create improving cash value.

Southwest Airlines[iv] is extremely successful, due in large part to their people strategy. Their employees are treated as their #1 asset. They are empowered to make changes on the spot as they recognize the need. People at Southwest take a lot of pride in what they do and are hardworking and dedicated. They are treated with dignity and respect and their suggestions for improvements are listened to. Employees will go out of their way to ensure that their customers are satisfied. Also, they are team players and assist each other when there is a need. It is not unusual for a Southwest Airline pilot to carry baggage, when the need exists.

In addition, Southwest has an excellent strategy. Their entire fleet is made up of one type of aircraft, Boeing 737s. This permits the pilots to be able to fly any of the Southwest aircraft, with little or no additional flight training. Inventory is kept at a minimum since most of the spare parts can be used on all the planes, regardless of any new model changes. Also, mechanics can repair the aircraft faster and with less training required than their competitors, since they are all 737s. Employees all assist each other to turn Southwest flights at the gate as quickly as is possible. Airlines are people movers, and the goal is to fill the aircraft to capacity and fly it 24 hours a day, 7 days a week or as close to that goal as is possible in order to create value. Southwest provides value to their customers with extremely competitive pricing, availability of flights when the customer requires them and excellent treatment of customers by their empowered employees. This allows Southwest to continually create positive cash flow value and economic profit.

CHAPTER III

Develop and Execute a Profitable Growth Plan

Process management, orders, backlog, deliveries, market share plan

A method that can be used to continuously improve the business is to implement process-based management as a normal way of doing business. In order to accomplish this, you should first map out the process. Included in this mapping you must define, flowchart and measure the current process. It is important that you map the process as it is currently being accomplished by the employees, not how you think it is being done based on current flow charts. You then need to analyze the process to determine activities being performed that are non-value added and that need to be eliminated.

The next step is to implement process improvements

to eliminate the non-value-added activities. Then you should evaluate and validate that that these activities have been eliminated. Finally, you should document the improvement that you have realized which is creating value for the company and update your process map to show that the non-value activities have been eliminated. Continuous improvement of processes is a way of life in world class companies.

In order to create value with orders, deliveries (revenue), and backlog there must be a sales and operations planning process in place that maintains a valid, current operating plan in support of customer requirements and the business plan. This process should include a monthly review and cover a planning horizon adequate to plan resources accordingly. In addition processes should be in place for the following:

Accountable Forecasting Process—There must be a process in place for forecasting all anticipated demands with sufficient detail and adequate planning horizons to support a formal planning and scheduling system which will help ensure that the product/service that has been ordered will be delivered to the customer on time when the order is due. Delivery must occur on the date requested by the customer. This system consists of business planning, sales and operations planning, and master production scheduling.

Some companies, such as Ford[v], have improved their

systems to the point that delivery to customers must occur not only on the date, but the time required on the receiving dock. This is known as "windows shipping." An example of how this works is as follows: The customer sends a receiving schedule to the company stating the time that the shipment is to be at the receiving dock. The schedule is usually for one week and can cover multiple products and shipments per day.

The supplier, with the help of the trucking company, factors in travel time, loading time, and a safety time and determines the time that the shipment is to be made. Multiple customers are all arranged the same way and the supplier comes up with a daily loading schedule. This usually works best with a steady schedule.

Advantages of " windows shipping" are:

Little or no additional inventory is required by the customer.

Live deliveries become the norm. The truck is backed up to the receiving dock and immediately unloaded. This frees up the truck for more hauling and saves freight costs. Extra shipping equipment is unnecessary. Round trips are a known factor due to live deliveries. Trucking companies know the shipping schedules and can plan accordingly. All of this amounts to a reduction in freight costs that can benefit the supplier and the customer and create cash value.

Production schedules can reflect receiving schedules.

This is the ultimate in a just-in-time environment.

In order for this to work properly the following must occur:

Each weeks schedule must be firm.

The customer must take what is ordered at the time they asked to receive it.

Any lost production must be adjusted in the following week's schedule.

A safety factor has to be incorporated to allow for a truck being late for any reason.

Sales plan—There must be a formal sales planning process in place with the sales force responsible and accountable for developing and executing the resulting sales plan. Differences between the sales plan and the forecast are reconciled.

Customer order entry plan—customer order entry should be integrated with the master production scheduling system and inventory data. Processes should be put in place for matching incoming orders to forecasts and for handling abnormal demands.

Master production scheduling—The master production scheduling process should be perpetually managed in order to ensure a balance of stability and responsiveness. The master production schedule should be reconciled with the production plan resulting from the sales and operations planning process.

Material planning and control—There should be a material planning process in place that maintains valid schedules and a material control process that communicates priorities through a manufacturing schedule, dispatch list or supplier schedule.

Supplier planning and control—A supplier planning and scheduling process provide visibility for key items covering an adequate planning horizon.

Capacity planning and control—There must be a capacity planning process using rough-cut capacity planning and, where applicable, capacity requirements planning in which planned capacity, based on demonstrated output, is balanced with required capacity. A capacity control process is used to measure and manage factory throughput and queues. Based on utilizing lean manufacturing/service techniques which include a planning and control process, improving cycle times and first pass quality, the product/service should flow through the factory quicker and the product/service should be delivered on-time per the customer-required delivery date, with zero defects. This will generate significant improvements in customer service and customer satisfaction, productivity, inventory reductions, and operational efficiency gains which will result in cost reductions, and lead to profitable growth due to increased orders and market share from satisfied customers.

You should provide competitive pricing, in addition to on-time delivery and zero defects, to your customers but should not buy market share if you can't create value with the price being offered. Your goal should always be profitable growth.

A backlog of orders is healthy as long as you ship/provide service to your customers when they require the product/service. In some industries, such as airplane manufacturing, a three-year backlog of airplane orders is not uncommon. In the sheave, sprocket and screw conveyor business, a two-week backlog is more the norm. A customer may call in the morning and tell you that they will send a truck over by late afternoon to pick up parts that they require. If you don't have a balanced and accurate inventory you will lose the business because they will purchase from your competitor.

Also, with a two-week backlog, it is more difficult to forecast what your sales will be for the month. That is why sales plans must constantly be reviewed and adjusted accordingly.

Finally, it is important to remember that you must have an order before you can create value. If you understand your markets and provide products/services that your customers find valuable, they will place orders with you, but you must ship the product or provide the service to create revenue and if you do not collect the resultant accounts receivable you will not create cash value since you will have to write off the sale as a bad debt.

Research and development plan

In order to create value you must continually invest in Research and Development for new and redesigned or re-engineered products/services whose value to the company will exceed the cost of capital. This is important to the continuous improvement process for the company and to achievement of the strategic and tactical profitable growth and cash flow stretch targets.

All functions in the organization must be involved with and actively support the product and service development process. Product and service requirements are derived from customer needs. Products and services must be developed in significantly shorter time periods, by reducing cycle times, in order to meet the customer requirements on a timely basis and require little or no support. Too long of a development process to have the best product/service could work against you and be the enemy of a good process that will get you to market quicker and provide the value to your customers that they are seeking. You could then work on product or service improvements that will provide additional value to your customers in the future. Multifunctional product development teams—including manufacturing, marketing, finance, quality assurance, purchasing, suppliers, and, where appropriate, customers should be used during the design process; also, design for manufacturability and concurrent engineering processes must be utilized at the beginning and throughout the product development process. All phases of new product development, including activities in support of a customer order, when applicable, must be integrated with the planning and control system. An effective process for re-engineering must also be in place for evaluating, planning and controlling changes to existing products and services.

An example of a process that could be used for new products/service and change to existing products and service is as follows:

1. Concept phase—Identify the opportunity, ensure strategic alignment with your business strategy, develop a preliminary business case analysis, including a business plan and financial plan and proceed if the projected earnings and cash flow value exceeds your cost of capital.

2. Evaluation phase—Define and exercise a prototype and pilot; develop a comprehensive business case and business plan, including marketing, pricing, and financials. The decision to proceed is based on the results of the evaluation of the prototype product/service and pilot exercise, market analysis, and finalized comprehensive business and financial plans and strategy fit.

3. Commitment phase— The final go/no go decision is based on the new business opportunity, business case analysis, and the overall strategy fit.

4. Production phase—Implement the project and transition it to the appropriate business unit. Conduct project daily management of metrics, etc. to ensure that the project is progressing as planned.

An ongoing effort to decrease the time-to-market, the elapsed time between the start of the design and the first shipment of the product or providing the new service is viewed as an important competitive weapon. This should be highly visible and measured, as success in this area will generate improvements to cash flow by the constant elimination of non-value-added activities.

The resulting revenue and margins or cost savings productivity improvements must satisfy the projections of the original plan proposals and yield returns greater than the cost of capital.

When reviewing a company's financial performance you should always analyze the income statement to see how much the company is spending on their research and development efforts. A rule of thumb in this area is at least 3% of revenue. If there is a substantial reduction in this area, then the company is attempting to maximize their short-term earnings and cash flow and is placing the long-term value of the company at substantial risk. No company can survive for very long without continual re-investment in research and development for new products/services and re-engineering of existing products/services to make them more competitive and to continue to provide what your customer requires as value to them.

Cycle time improvement plan

Cycle time is viewed as the amount of time between the start of the design and the first shipment of the product or providing the service for new and redesigned products/services and from when you receive the order to when you ship the product or provide the service based on the customer-required date.

Reduced cycle time or flow time is extremely important to the goal of creating cash value, since the longer a product takes to manufacture or the longer it takes you to provide the service ordered, the more costly it will be to you in the form of increased material, labor and overhead costs.

In order to have a world class company, you should encourage initiatives that eliminate non-value-added activity and that reduce cycle time and improve quality in all your value-added processes that are part of your business, product/service, production and people strategy.

Stretch targets should be established for the continual reduction of cycle time or flow time.

An ideal stretch target for product cycle time would be that you would receive the material for the product in the morning and produce the product and ship it to the customer by the end of the day. For a service, you would receive the order in the morning and complete the service the same day.

By attaining one day cycle times for your products and services you will improve cash flows and economic profit which creates value for the company.

Quality improvement plan

The quality of the product or service provided to the customer must be world class in the customer's perception. Nothing else counts. For world class companies or organizations, quality first means providing total quality products and/or services for customers is the primary business policy that must be adhered to. Actions should be taken to guarantee the highest quality for customers, before cutting costs and capital investments to attempt to shore up short-term profits. Only a long-term quality focus, not a short-term profit orientation, achieves long-term competitiveness and resulting long-term earnings and cash value improvements; therefore, the quality-first policy can never be compromised.

Quality at world class companies or organizations is never second to cost reduction or attaining schedule performance. Quality is a measure of the integrity of a company and, as such, can never be compromised if you hope to achieve the respect of your customers and competitors. At world class companies, all empowered employees in the organization are committed to and comply with and ensure the practice of total quality in all areas of the business, office as well as factory. Routine use of the basic tools of total quality control and the practice of mistake proofing must become a way of life in virtually all areas of the company.

Short- and long-term quality goals that cause the organization to stretch are established, regularly reviewed, and monitored. These goals are targeted on improvements in total cost, cycle time (or response time) and customer quality requirements.

Suppliers must be required to deliver products or

services to you with zero defects that require no additional inspection on your part. Cycle time must be reduced to the point of the elimination of all non-value-added activities, and employees must all be properly trained, empowered, and rewarded to be motivated to produce a product or service with zero defects. The goal should be to develop a first pass quality system with zero defects by building the quality in and not inspecting it in.

Employees should be encouraged and rewarded for Six Sigma quality behavior that contributes to the attainment of customer product or service quality satisfaction and the attainment of the company cash flow projections. Six Sigma quality is defined as three defects per million units processed. This could represent shipments, documents, operations, etc. and is considered a world class measurement of excellence. Motorola[vi] was one of the first companies to attain this goal and was a recipient of the Malcolm Baldridge national award for quality excellence for their products. This enabled Motorola to become a premier manufacturing company.

Some of the benefits of a total quality system are reduced scrap, rework and warranty costs and improved material, labor and overhead costs as a result of operational efficiencies that are created due to zero defects of your product or service. This in turn leads to improved value and cash flow target attainment.

Suppliers material/service plan

In most manufacturing companies, on the average, material costs represent 50%+ of total costs and in service companies 25%+ of total costs. With this in mind, it becomes extremely important in value creation to work with your suppliers as partners to provide you inventory on time based on your requirement date that has first pass quality built in and that is competitively priced. The procurement process should be continuously improved and simplified to improve quality and responsiveness while simultaneously reducing the total procurement costs. Strong partnership relationships that are mutually beneficial should be established with fewer but better suppliers, to facilitate improvements in quality, cost and overall responsiveness. Utilizing the 80/20 rule as a guide, 20% of your suppliers should provide you 80% of your inventory/service. As partners, suppliers should also be asked for their input when you are designing a new product/service or redesigning an old product/service. They should also be given feedback on their performance as your valued supplier on the following:

Supplier measures—Measure:

1. On-time delivery performance to you based on your requirements of when you require the delivery.

2. Defects-quality performance. All products /services delivered to you should have zero defects and require no inspection on your part.

3. Cost performance—All products/services contracted for delivery to you should be extremely competitively priced.

4. Customer satisfaction—Your suppliers should be given feedback on your satisfaction with their products/ services and scored accordingly.

In order to provide suppliers with accurate schedule information so that they can deliver raw material and parts (just in time) when you require the inventory/service you must have an accurate formal planning and scheduling system in place that is at least 95% + accurate. This process is used for forecasting all anticipated demands with sufficient detail and an adequate planning horizon to support business planning, sales and operations planning, and master production scheduling.

Material planning and control—There should be a material planning process in place that maintains valid schedules and a material control process that communicates priorities through a manufacturing schedule, dispatch list or supplier schedule.

Supplier planning and control—A supplier planning and scheduling process is used to provide visibility for key items covering an adequate planning horizon.

Bills of material and routings should be at least 98% accurate so that forecast demands for material truly represent what it will take to produce the product/service.

You should order inventory/services working with suppliers to deliver raw material and parts when you require the inventory. Provide long-term supplier agreements as blanket orders to your suppliers as an incentive to provide you shipments on the day you require the inventory.

In order to ensure that material required is available, point of use storage bins (child bins) can be co-located in an on-floor cell and be replenished as part of a kanban pull system. When inventory of a part is depleted, demand is transferred to a main storage bin (mother bin) where the stock is replenished. This then creates demand for a re-order of parts, as required.

This requirement of just-in-time inventory delivery to you becomes critical to your success of creating value as you continue to reduce cycle times and work off your excess inventory. The time required to manufacture products must be reduced such that the planning and control system uses forecasts to project material and capacity needs, but production of finished products is based on actual customer orders or distribution demands (except where strategic or seasonal inventories are being built. If suppliers do not deliver the inventory on the required date it will disrupt your total process and add waste and costs to your product or service.

Since you are giving your suppliers firm long-term agreements, you should also insist that the inventory/service have first pass quality built in and require no inspection on your part in order to use the raw material or purchased parts in your finished product. This requirement will minimize or eliminate scrap/rework due to poor supplier quality as you utilize the inventory/service delivered to you.

Employment Plan

In most manufacturing companies, labor costs are generally 25%+ of total costs, while in service companies labor can run 50%+ of total costs. As you progress towards becoming a world class organization and productivity improves, you should require fewer employees to produce the same or greater goods and services. Employment continuity is an important goal as long as the employee exceeds the minimum acceptable job requirements and the level of business is viable.

You should utilize people as an asset and permit them

to make a difference in the creation of value. You must also provide and ensure that there is an active education and training process in place for all employees. Its objectives should include continuous improvement, enhancing the empowered worker, teamwork, flexibility, employment stability and meeting future needs.

You should attempt to minimize hiring and layoffs. This is extremely expensive and is a morale and productivity issue as you are continually training new employees and providing severance pay for your laid-off employees. One way to minimize hiring and layoffs is to staff to the current business plan assuming 5% to 8% overtime will be required. This is much less expensive than planning on no overtime. With additional people and no overtime you are paying fringe benefits, which in most companies' amount to 40-60% of your labor costs and you are in a constant layoff and hiring mode when your business demands change. This increases your training costs, and also costs you when there is a layoff and you provide a severance package. In addition, more people means higher overhead costs for computer work stations, supplies, etc.

As your people make continuous improvements and improve value creation in your company you can reduce overtime and cut costs which will make you more competitive and permit you to create more profitable growth, which creates additional jobs and provides employees with greater job security.

In a lean company material requirements will be forecasted properly and raw material and parts required will arrive when needed with zero defects. Continual training and retraining of employees when working with first pass quality material will result in less rework and scrap costs. The company will have a capacity planning process in place using rough-cut capacity planning and, where applicable, capacity requirements planning in which planned capacity, based on demonstrated output, is balanced with required capacity. The capacity control process is used to measure and manage factory throughput and queues. Also, cycle times will have been reduced to the point where little if any time buffers are left between operations. A point to consider is that the longer jobs sit in the factory the more cost is added as additional labor and material costs. As non-value added processes and waste are eliminated, the process is streamlined and productivity increases in the office and factory. Improved salary and hourly productivity means that less people, overtime, and fringe benefits are required to produce and deliver the same or increased products and services. This translates into additional savings and improved cash value.

Safety Plan

An important part of your creating value strategy is to provide a safe and effective work place for employees. Safety should be an integral part of all your activities and should never be compromised. Employees should be properly trained and expected to exhibit safe behavior at all times.

As you measure and improve your lost workday case rate you will improve morale and productivity, because employees will know that the company is serious about safe behavior. As employee lost workdays are reduced due to fewer accidents, cash flow will increase as a result of reduced worker's compensation costs and improved productivity. You then will not require as many employees to cover for employees not at work due to lost time injuries, which improves your operational efficiency and cash flow due to reductions in labor costs and fringe benefits.

One example of an excellent safety program was a company in Irving, Texas, where electronic modules were manufactured for Boeing aircraft and shipped to Seattle, Washington, to be assembled on the airplanes. Electronic modules require much hand assembly work that can lead to carpal tunnel repetitive motion injuries. One of the first things done to reduce these injuries was to purchase special ergonomic tools that fit perfectly into the hands of the assemblers. In addition, ergonomic chairs were purchased for all employees that could be adjusted up, down, back and forward, depending on a worker's size. This was useful for office workers, also, in preventing injuries.

Work stations were then modified so that the work benches could be adjusted up or down, depending on the stature of the assembler. During shift changes, the new worker would come in and adjust the work station and chair to their comfort level.

Ergonomic exercises were also required of all employees for six minutes at the start of each shift. These were done by each department and were fun and useful in reducing injuries. This also helped in promoting teamwork. Employees were also encouraged to exercise during their shift, doing thumb stretches, neck rolls, etc., as required.

The result of all these preventative injury actions resulted in a major reduction in lost workday case rate hours and worker's compensation claims, which amounted to over $1,000,000 a year in cost savings and improving cash value.

Employees' morale also improved, because they felt that the company cared about them as people and was concerned about their health and safety. This all translated into improved productivity.

Diversity Plan

In order to have a world class company you should emphasize diversity in your workforce and actively recruit so this becomes a fact. A diverse workforce could be a competitive advantage for you if utilized properly. You should listen to your people's ideas and take advantage of the diverse group employed by you.

Ethics Plan

World class companies and organizations must always maintain an environment of the highest ethical standards, without exception.

Proper "ethical business conduct" requires that all employees conduct business fairly, impartially, in an ethical and proper manner, and in full compliance with all laws and regulations. Responsibility for the company's commitment to integrity rests with each employee.

The purpose of an ethics and business conduct program is to communicate to employees the company's or organization's commitment to integrity and to inform them of the company standards of conduct. A published code of ethics must be adhered to by all employees and should include a program that provides resources and communication channels for resolving questions and concerns, including a means for reporting suspected violations, separate from line management.

Excellent management leadership is required to ensure company wide consistency regarding ethics policies, issues, and ethics and business conduct training which should be conducted each year as required training for all employees.

Proper ethical conduct shall be values based and governed by your integrity as a fundamental part of the way you do business. Your commitment to integrity means that all of your actions and relationships are based on these uncompromising values.

1. Report current and future projected earnings and cash flows that reflect the true performance of the company and are not merely the result of creative accounting techniques.

2. Comply with all federal, state and local laws and regulations.

3. Treat each other with respect.

4. Deal fairly in all of your relationships.

5. Honor your commitments and obligations

6. Communicate openly and honestly.

7. Take responsibility for your actions.

8. Deliver safe and reliable products/services of the highest quality.

9. Provide equal opportunity for all.

Since a company/organization is its people and everything accomplished in a company/organization is a result of actions by those people, it behooves you to provide and maintain an environment of the highest ethical standards if you are truly to be world class.

Internal and external pressure to continually increase shareholder value should never cause you to do anything that is unethical or illegal. Reported earnings after taxes, earnings per share and cash flow must always reflect how the company/organization is actually performing. Using creative accounting to distort current and forecasted earnings is unethical and illegal. A recent example of this was when some major corporations were capitalizing their expenses and depreciating them over the life of their capital equipment rather than showing these costs as current period costs in order to inflate current earnings and shareholder value so that the value of the company and their stock options would be higher than they deserved to be. This overinflated the value of the company and caused investors to purchase more stock based on earnings reports that were fraudulent. When this was discovered it led to the collapse of these companies and the loss of millions of dollars of stock value for investors that had been planning on this money as part of their retirement funds and for many other purposes. This is just one example of what can happen when greed takes over and proper ethical business behavior becomes just a set of words and is not practiced by all employees in a business/organization.

Overhead Plan

In most companies overhead represents 25% or more of total cost. Some examples of overhead costs are: indirect labor, fringe benefits, overtime, computer support (hardware and software), supplies, travel, maintenance of the building, grounds and equipment, depreciation expense, taxes, utilities, training, hazardous waste disposal, recycling, clean environmental programs, etc.

Companies usually classify overhead as variable, semi-variable and fixed. Variable and semi-variable should be adjusted up or down,depending on your forecasted and actual sales volume in relationship to the planned volume that the original budgets were based on. As volumes increase or decrease, variable and semi-variable overhead costs must be adjusted to reflect the volume change. In total, costs should remain variable to volume, but individual processes and cost centers might have to be adjusted greater or less than the volume change in order to continue to create value with the amount of overhead that is affordable. In some companies you are asked to reduce variable overhead when volume decreases and not allow the variable overhead to increase in relationship to any volume increase. This philosophy might work in the short term; especially if your overhead budgets have some excess costs incorporated in them, but will hamper you in the long-term creation of value as you attempt to grow the business.

As you become a lean organization and reduce cycle time and improve quality and on-time supplier delivery of parts, you will reduce direct labor costs, which means that you will require less indirect or support labor, which will reduce your indirect labor and fringe costs.

Reduced labor in your support functions means that you will require less computer support, supplies, travel, etc.

Care for the environment is an integral factor in the way you should plan and conduct your business. Processes and materials that are used in production or to provide a service should always avoid, reduce or control pollution. This may actually cause some of your overhead costs to increase, but you must always comply with government laws and regulations concerning care for the environment, and should consider these costs as a necessary cost of doing business.

As you continue to improve cycle time and quality and eliminate non-value added activities, less office and factory space and equipment will be required to support current production or service functions. Selling or leasing this excess space and equipment will reduce your fixed costs and will improve earnings and cash flow value by reducing taxes, utilities, and fixed depreciation expense.

Unit Cost Plan

As you become a world class lean company/organization with elimination of waste, reduction of cycle times, improved first pass quality and on-time delivery of parts by your suppliers and to your customers, you must also have a world class cost system that will give you true, accurate cost information on your units and finished products or services. Activity-based costing as well as other costing methodologies must be understood, and the most suitable costing method should be used. This cost system must provide total cost visibility to the organizational unit, identify cost drivers and relevant data to promote continuous improvement, support cost reduction activities in material, labor and overhead costs, link costs to the way work is truly being accomplished, and complement customer quality and schedule performance expectations if you are to be successful in value creation.

As you experience greater than 95%+ accuracy in your schedules, inventory balances, bills of material and quality, your unit costs will continue to improve. Accounting procedures and paperwork should be simplified, eliminating non-value-added activities, while at the same time providing the ability to generate product costs sufficiently accurate to use in decision making and satisfy audit requirements.

You should put in place a cost system that allows you to direct charge materials and labor to the unit or service that is being produced. In addition, overhead should be charged based on the process or activity that is being performed to the unit. In many cases some units require much more engineering, service, sales and other overhead support and should be charged with a higher overhead rate than a more simplistic product or service.

By providing more accurate unit costs and finished product costs that are updated daily, if required, you will be able to make more intelligent business decisions on the contribution to the company or organization's earnings and cash flow value based on extremely accurate product or service profit and loss statements that show the contribution to the bottom line of all your major products and services.

In order to properly value your inventory, you might want to consider also having a standard cost system based on your constantly updated unit costs. The standard cost system could be updated two to three times a year, as required, based on any major cost changes that might occur. The updated standard costs could then be used to re-evaluate and re-cost your inventory for financial purposes.

As you continue to improve your operational efficiency for material, labor and overhead costs by eliminating non-value-added activities and improving cycle time and quality, you will reduce costs and improve earnings/margins. This will permit selling prices to be adjusted where necessary to be more competitive and will lead to profitable growth, which will increase the cash flow value of the company.

CHAPTER IV DEVELOP AND EXECUTE AN ASSET AND CAPITAL UTILIZATION PLAN

Asset utilization plan—Customer advances

By creating value for your customers as partners you can ask for cash advances as you receive orders for products/services. This will help you maximize your cash flow and provide you cash to use for capital and Research and Development investment opportunities. In addition, by receiving some of the cash due to you up front, you will have cash available to start the job and pay for some of your material, labor and overhead costs that you will incur.

An example of this is Boeing. When Boeing receives an order for a new airplane they generally ask for one-third cash deposit. The second third of the monies is due when the order is started and the final third is due when the order is delivered.

In most service businesses you order the service and payment is due when the service is complete, in cash or by credit card. This method also maximizes your cash flow, since payment is received as soon as the service is performed. However, this can backfire on you if you are not performing a high-quality service and the customer is not satisfied. In this case the customer may choose to withhold payment until the service is completed to their satisfaction.

Asset Utilization Plan—Accounts Receivable

In the overall plan of value creation you must receive an order for goods or services before you can begin to create value. Then you must deliver the goods or services ordered to your customers on time based on their required delivery date and the product or service must be of superior quality with zero defects to be acceptable to the customer.

This will enable you to experience profitable growth but will not necessarily lead you to the creation of cash flow value. In order to experience positive cash flow you must collect your accounts receivable when due from your customers. Many companies relax when they ship the product or provide the service and leave it to their finance organizations to assume the responsibility of collecting the accounts receivable due.

Until you collect the accounts receivable due, you have not truly created any value. If you experience a bad debt, you will have to write off the accounts receivable, which will have a negative impact on your earnings and cash flow.

In a world class company you must be partners with your customers from the order creation through delivery of the product or service and finally through the payment of the invoice due.

In some cases this may take creativity in working out financing arrangements with your customer when your customer experiences unplanned financial difficulties. You must continually remember that you and your customers are partners and both of you must be successful in order to create value. Writing off a receivable as a bad debt is not a win-win for you or your customer. Your ultimate goal is to create positive cash flow for both of you.

Asset Utilization Plan – Inventory

In most companies, inventory represents one of your largest investments and, as such, presents you with one of your greatest opportunities to more effectively utilize your inventory asset and improve your cash flow.

Some companies work under the theory that more of everything is better. This is known as just-in-case inventory. A machine tool company in Fort Worth, Texas, operated this way for many years. The owner wanted to make certain that when a customer called and ordered a part, the part would always be available for immediate delivery or pick-up. In theory this made sense, but many of the parts that were being carried in inventory were not turning and were eventually being written off the books as zero usage and excess inventory and were disposed of. This was waste and did nothing to improve cash flow value. In addition, there were still instances where certain parts that customers required were not available because the company did not have a good forecast system and kept parts in stock only based on historical demand.

As you become a lean production or service company and develop a world class material or manufacturing resource planning system by improving your cycle times and quality and becoming partners with your suppliers to provide you just-in-time quality inventory based on a forecast system that anticipates customer demand, you will be able to reduce excess inventory and keep zero usage inventory to a minimum. Also, as part of this process improvement, you must have an inventory control process in place that provides accurate warehouse, stockroom, and work-in-process inventory data. At least 95% of all item inventory records must match the physical counts, within the counting tolerance.

This will permit you to constantly increase inventory turns which are measured as yearly cost of sales divided by average inventory. An example of what this could mean is as follows:

If you have a $100,000 inventory and are turning it two times a year and can double your turns to four times a year you would only require $50,000 in inventory to ship the same product or provide the same service. This would permit you to have available an additional $50,000 in cash to invest in new or redesigned products or services and capital that will create value for you. In addition, as you improve the management of your inventory, you will reduce the possibility of having to write-off and dispose of zero usage and excess inventory which reduces your earnings and company value.

Continual profitable growth re-investment in the business will create more earnings and add to company value.

Current Liabilities – Accounts Payable

Suppliers are to be treated as partners in all your endeavors, including on time payments based on agreed to terms. Extending payments to suppliers to maximize your cash flow does little to develop trust and in treating them as partners. Your goal should be to create value for them. One way to accomplish this is to pay their invoices when they are due. They need their positive cash flow to be successful in value creation so that they can continue to be a key partner and successful supplier to you for goods and services required.

Working Capital = Current assets less Current Liabilities

Working Capital is the amount of cash liquidity that you possess from your cash on hand, through customer advances, what you can collect from accounts receivable, and the amount you can cash in from improved inventory turnover, less what you owe in current liabilities, such as accounts payable. Improved asset utilization will result in improved working capital, which when properly invested will create value.

Asset Utilization Plan—Facilities/Equipment

As you continue to progress towards a lean production or service environment by continually reducing your cycle times, improving your first pass quality and reducing your inventory balances you will require less facilities/equipment for the current business stream and the plant can be rearranged to make it more efficient. Resources and facilities required to economically receive, produce and ship or provide the product or service should continuously be made more flexible, cost effective and capable of producing improved quality.

Excess facilities and equipment could be sold or sub-leased creating additional other income and cash flow. Underutilized equipment could be sold and you could study possible sub-contracting for the part required, which may be less expensive than producing it and create value.

Reduced facilities/equipment means reduced depreciation expense, if sold, and reduced utilities, taxes, etc., which reduces your overhead costs and increases your earnings.

In a world class company it is important to ensure the availability of all machines/equipment at all times. Downtime adds costs to the product or service and reduces operational efficiency and earnings. Also, downtime could impact the agreed to delivery schedule to the customer and their value creation. High-performing factories use programs like "total preventative maintenance" to involve operators in the day-to-day maintenance of equipment. Operators must accept ownership of their equipment and take all actions necessary to complete preventative maintenance schedules 95%+ on time and to accomplish the proper amount of preventative maintenance for achievement of 100% availability of all equipment. This objective should be noted on all operators' performance management each year, and satisfactory accomplishment should be recognized and rewarded accordingly, when achieved.

Another area of high impact to costs and cycle time is associated with "set-up times." In the traditional definition, set-up reduction is focused on the fabrication processes. Reducing the time allows for smaller production cost, which is the desired effect in contributing to a lean environment, enabling just-in-time production and low inventory levels. Expanding the set-up time reduction to focus on reducing or eliminating non-value-added time and people, in all aspects of manufacturing, enables a much more powerful application of this concept that will have significant impact on reducing costs, improving quality and performing on schedule. An example of this is reducing the number of employees necessary to perform the set-up (utilizing click-in-place tooling has been very effective in accomplishing this). The Japanese automobile industry was one of the first to perfect this technique, and the American automobile industry followed suit. Instead of running 50,000 parts at a time due to the high cost of set-up of the tools and dies, you would now run only the parts required based on your current forecast and reduce the amount of excess inventory that you are carrying, which increases your cash flow value. Other examples are reducing the number of times a part has to be touched through improved container concepts and resequencing operations to allow for one set-up of the same size hole rather than several set-ups, etc.

In summary, more efficient use of your facilities and equipment will go a long way towards assisting you in the creation of value.

Develop and execute a capital plan

Creating value considers the following:

Companies are truly profitable and create value if an only if their income generated exceeds the cost of all the capital they use to finance operations. Until a company returns a profit greater than its cost of capital, it operates at a loss in the creation of value, despite the fact that it pays taxes on earnings that it has generated.

If a company returns less than the cost of what it uses in resources, it does not create wealth –it destroys it. Your plan for new products/services, redesign of existing products/services, plant expansions of existing facilities and construction of new plants and purchase of new equipment must be tested first for congruence to the business strategy and must generate tactical and strategic planned returns on sales that are greater than your cost of the capital required in order for you to continually create cash flow value and economic profit.

For example, if the cost of capital to you was 10%, then you must generate returns on your investments of greater than 10% to create positive economic profits.

CHAPTER V EXPERIENCE FAVORABLE PERFORMANCE AND VALUE CREATION

Performance—Profitable Growth

By continuing to work with your customers as partners and providing them with products and services that provide value to them, that are delivered to them when required, have zero defects, and are competitively priced, you will experience profitable growth with increased orders, deliveries, and higher market share.

Performance—Operational Efficiency

As you continue to reduce your cycle times, improve your first pass quality, utilize your team-based culture and people strategy where people are trained, empowered, treated with dignity, trust and respect and are recognized and rewarded for attainment of initiatives that tie in to the company strategic objectives, strategy and vision and that eliminate waste, you will experience improvements in your operational efficiency which will lower your costs and improve margins and earnings.

Performance—Asset Utilization

As you continue to utilize your assets more effectively, most notably by reducing your inventory and changing the culture of the company to a just-in-time inventory environment with little, if any, excess and zero usage inventory, and fully utilizing your facilities and equipment so that there is very little wasted factory and office space, and that all equipment is being used to maximum capacity you will free up additional capital that can be invested to further profitably grow the business.

Economic Profit—Value Creation

One calculation that you can make to determine if you are utilizing your assets is to calculate economic profit. This is equal to earnings less corporate taxes (35%), equals after tax earnings, less a capital charge of approximately 5% -15% of your average net assets depending on the current cost of capital. Economic profit should always be positive if you have positive earnings and if you are utilizing your assets properly.

Return on net assets (RONA) is calculated as operating earnings divided by average net assets. As this percent increases, you will increase economic profit because you will be utilizing your assets in a more efficient manner.

Asset turns is calculated as cost of sales divided by average net assets—Improved turns here also helps increase economic profit. This would be the result of reduced assets required such as accounts receivable, inventory and facilities and equipment due to utilizing continuous improvement creating value techniques.

Cash flow—Value creation

The net result of increased earnings and economic profit will be increased cash flow. As earnings per share (net earnings after tax divided by number of shares outstanding) and actual cash flow discounted for inflation, which is the net present value of cash, equals or exceeds the forecasted cash flows, shareholder value—defined as shares of stock outstanding times stock market price should continue to increase.

This should all be the positive result of your strategic planning processes and operating performance measurements that are aligned with or directly focused on enhancing long-term shareholder value.

Continuous improvement—value creation

World class companies or organizations have a passion for continuous improvement even when they are leading the pack and in those organizations continuous improvement is a way of life as they strive to understand, control, improve their processes and eliminate waste in order to achieve full customer satisfaction. A formal program is used to expose, prioritize, and stimulate the elimination of non-value-added activities. These companies understand that how processes are managed and performed has a direct bearing upon the success of the organization and its leverage over competitors. Processes that are smoothly integrated and continually reviewed for value-added content, simplification and applicability to the needs of internal and external customers will provide a higher-quality and lower-cost product or service in a shorter period of time.

The objective of process thinking at world class companies or organizations is to improve the effectiveness and efficiency of processes by using the knowledge of involved employees to satisfy the customer. Effectiveness means meeting customer requirements and expectations. Efficiency means doing so without wasting resources. Managing processes at world class companies or organizations involves measuring, coordinating, improving, and institutionalizing processes. It also involves the communication of information about the process, customers, and suppliers to all individuals who directly or indirectly affect the process.

In summary, continuous improvement initiatives must be a way of life in your company or organization as they will result in process improvements that will see continued reduction in non-value activities, defects, cycle times and inventory levels which will add up to decreased costs and improved quality of your products and services and play a major role in making and keeping you world class competitive.

CHAPTER VI CREATE CONTINUALLY IMPROVING CASH VALUE— SUMMARY

By creating value for your customers, suppliers, employees and investors and continuously improving on your profitable growth, operational efficiency and asset utilization you will be world class competitive and be the best manufacturing or service company in the world. In world class companies, continuous improvement is a way of life. Companies must target improved market share that is profitable in order to be successful. Also, costs must continually be properly managed at all levels of the organization, all non-value activities must be eliminated, and assets must be fully utilized. Companies must also embrace a creating value approach to accomplish this by maintaining a balanced value creation, which will ensure that your customers, suppliers, employees and investors are all successful.

These companies also agree that people are their #1 asset and their actions of treating people with dignity, trust and respect, communicating and listening to and empowering people to function in a team environment, to take responsibility for the company strategy and objectives and recognizing and rewarding them for their accomplishments will help ensure that they are creating maximum cash value for all.

In summary, if you totally understand your business environment, have a vision and strategy that are understood and embraced by all, have a world class plan to accomplish your goals and ensure that you are creating cash value for your customers, suppliers, employees and investors, you should experience continuous improvement and predictability in your forecasted and actual cash flows and positive economic profits and truly have a world class company or organization.

CREATING VALUE CHECKLIST – APPENDIX A

Utilize this appendix as a checklist for your company to determine if you are creating value for your customers, suppliers, employees and investors.

1. From a global perspective, it is the responsibility of management to maximize shareholder value, by leveraging the company's strengths and minimizing its weaknesses. Please identify your company's strengths and any deficiencies you feel might hinder your success and could contribute to the company's performance targets not being met?

2. In what ways does competition drive your business? Do you feel your company sets the pace for the competition?

3. What steps are you taking in your plan to make your company more valuable when faced with aggressive concessions from the competition?

4. How do you partner with your external and internal customers to provide them the products and services that will create value for them?

5. What is the vision and strategy for your company?

6. How do the company's product, service, and production strategy, if you are a manufacturing company, align with the business plan?

7. What are the value drivers of the business? Is it profitable revenue growth, operating margins or working capital?

8. Are objectives, measures, targets and initiatives in place to support the strategy?

9. What is your people strategy? Do you have a team-based culture? Are your employees empowered and rewarded and recognized for achievements? Do you utilize a performance management system?

10. What percentage of sales do you allocate to Research and Development expense?

11. How do you work with your suppliers? Are they partners in your business? Are they given firm schedules to support a just-in-time inventory that has first pass quality built in? Do your material costs reflect improved pricing with suppliers based on firm schedules? What percentage of your costs are materials? Do you measure supplier delivery performance as number of items received on time (within quantity and time tolerance) divided by number of orders due this week?

12. Have you developed a formal planning and scheduling system that will help ensure that the product is delivered to the customer on time? Do you measure customer delivery performance, which is number of items shipped on time (within quantity and time tolerance) divided by number of items due (as of original promise date)

13. Are you utilizing lean manufacturing and lean service techniques to continually improve on-time delivery, cycle times and quality? Do you measure velocity as value-added time divided by elapsed time?

14. Do you measure quality, which is (parts per million/defects per million parts, which could be shipments, documents, operations, etc.) =Defects x 1,000,000 divided by units processed. What is your targeted level of performance for quality? What are your scrap and rework rates?

15. How do you measure productivity improvements?

16. What is your overtime rate?

17. What is your fringe rate?

18. How do you measure safety? What are your workers' compensation costs?

19. How much do you spend on training per year, including training for proper ethical behavior?

20. What is your direct-to-indirect ratio of employees?

21. What percentage of your cost is labor?

22. What is your strategy to continually reduce variable and semi-variable overhead costs?

23. How will you identify, evaluate and implement projects/process improvements that meet or exceed your investor's expectations?

24. EVA (Economic Value Added) is used by some companies to evaluate and measure performance and in some cases to determine managerial bonuses. The idea behind EVA considers the economic question "companies are truly profitable and create value if and only if their income exceeds the cost of all the capital they use to finance operations." Are you currently involved in any projects that generated returns greater than their costs of capital? Can you elaborate on what types of projects these are and what makes these projects different from other projects your company is involved in?

25. What types of debt (bank loans, commercial paper, equity financing) do you typically use to finance your capital/business spending and why? What advantage is derived?

26. How does your company set capital spending targets?

27. What is your current target capital structure? Your mix of debt, preferred stock and common equity?

28. How do you evaluate cash flow, and when do you change your cash flow targets?

29. How do you calculate and manage your inventory turnover? Do you measure the accuracy of bills of material, routings and inventory count accuracy?

Bill of material accuracy is defined as *The number of correct bills (Auditing single-level parent number/component relationships, quantity per, and units of measure) divided by the total number of bills checked.*

Routing accuracy is defined as *The number of correct routings (Auditing work center identification, sequence of operations, and standards, within tolerance) divided by total number of routings checked.*

Inventory record accuracy is defined as *Number of correct items/quantities/locations divided by the number of items/quantities/locations checked.*

30. Do you age your inventory to determine possible excess and obsolete inventory?

31. Ensuring shareholder value is essential in publicly held companies. Can you describe your risk and opportunity assessment of present and future demands on capital?

Do you utilize the following calculations as a gauge on how the business is performing?

Return on sales = Net earnings after tax / by net sales

Operational efficiency = Operating earnings / by net sales

Orders/deliveries; Calculate market share improvement

Research and Development expense/ Net sales

Inventory turnover = Yearly cost of goods sold / average inventory

Return on net assets employed (RONA) = Operating earnings / average net assets

Asset turns = Yearly cost of goods sold / Average net assets

Cash flow = Net earnings +/- Change in net assets: When forecasting future cash flows, calculate the net present value of cash adjusted for inflation.

Free cash flow = Net earnings +/- non cash adj. (I.E. depreciation expense) = Cash earnings +/- change in working capital

Economic profit = After tax earnings less a capital charge of 7-10% of your net assets

NOTES

[i] National Machinery is a trademark of National Machinery Company

[ii] Boeing is a trademark of The Boeing Company

[iii] BMW is a trademark of Bayerische Motoren Werke Aktiengesellschaft

[iv] Southwest Airlines is a trademark of Southwest Airlines Company

[v] Ford is a trademark of Ford Motor Company

[vi] Motorola is a trademark of Motorola, Inc.

Printed in the United States
37746LVS00002B/4-57